Plant-Based Whole Food Recipes

Healthy Homemade Meals Made Easy

I0558357

Yu-Shiaw Chen, Ph.D.

ARPress
ILLUMINATING IDEAS,
EMPOWERING VOICES

ARPress LLC
45 Dan Road Suite 5
Canton MA 02021
Hotline: 1(888) 821-0229
Fax: 1(508) 545-7580

Ordering Information:
Quantity sales. Special discounts are available on quantity purchases by corporations, associations, and others. For details, contact the publisher at the address above.

Printed in the United States of America.

ISBN-13:	Softcover	979-8-89356-629-1
	Hardback	979-8-89356-630-7
	eBook	979-8-89356-631-4

Library of Congress Control Number: 2024903617

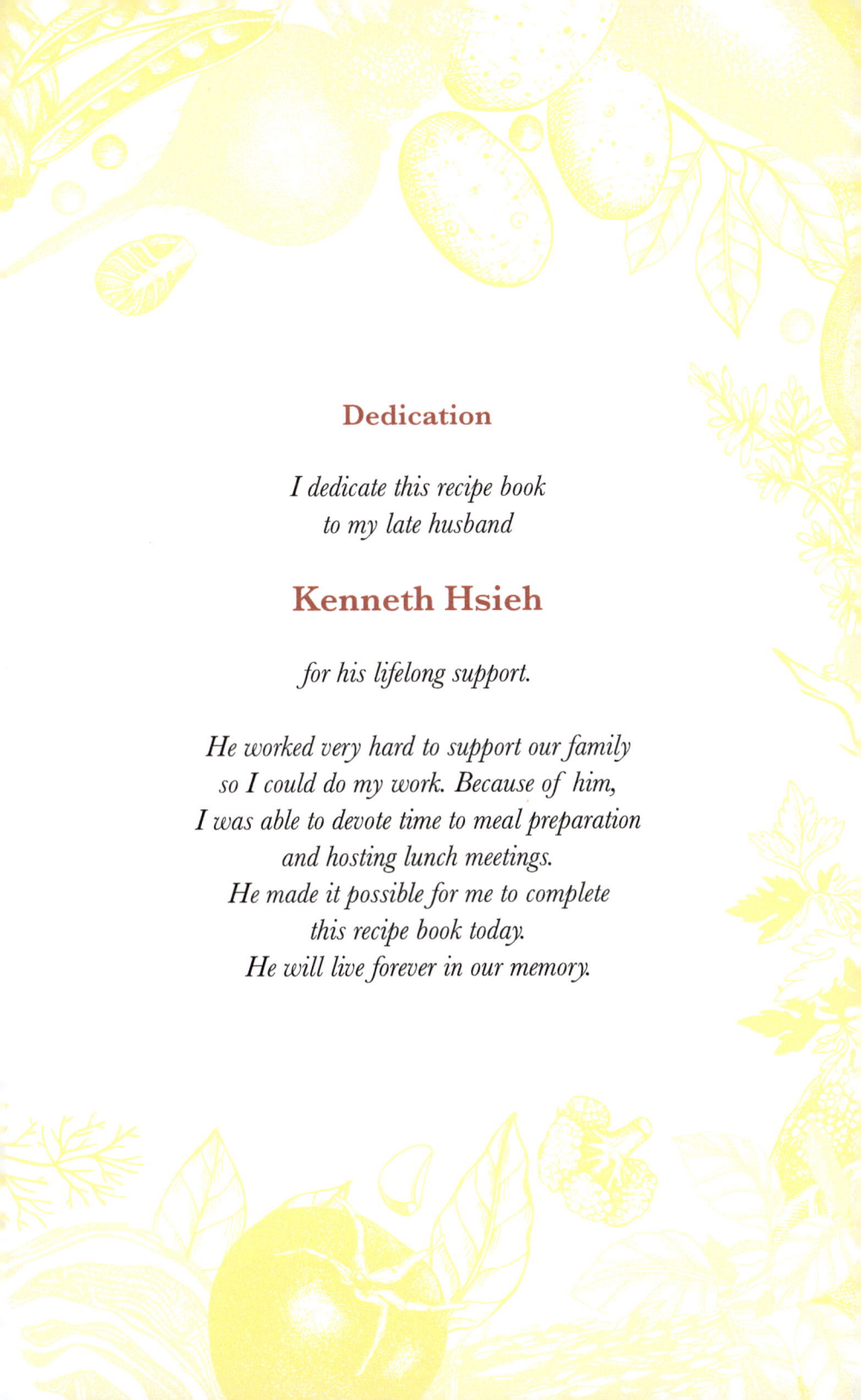

Dedication

I dedicate this recipe book
to my late husband

Kenneth Hsieh

for his lifelong support.

He worked very hard to support our family
so I could do my work. Because of him,
I was able to devote time to meal preparation
and hosting lunch meetings.
He made it possible for me to complete
this recipe book today.
He will live forever in our memory.

Plant-Based Whole Food Recipes
By Yu-Shiaw Chen, Ph.D.

This recipe book is written for health-conscious people who are too busy to make homemade meals or for people who are looking for new ideas to eat healthier. It will be good for anybody who is trying to lose weight; get rid of aches, pains, or fatigue; or anyone fighting disorders such as diabetes, heart disease, or cancer. A well-balanced diet will provide you with good nutrition, and nutrition is the foundation for our health and well-being.

There are five chapters in this book, from raw food to whole grains, to beans and legumes, to cooked vegetables and combination dishes. Each category has more than ten different recipes, and each recipe comes with a picture to make it clear. To begin with, the author explains the importance of having raw foods. The life enzymes in raw foods make the whole difference in nutrition. Besides ingredients and preparation, she touches the bases of nutrition or health benefits of some unfamiliar ingredients in each chapter. She shows you how to prepare a dozen breakfasts ahead of time, so you can have breakfast instantly before work every day.

The author introduces you to a few ingredients from Chinese or Asian culture, such as bitter melon, okra, lotus root, wood ear mushroom, shiitake mushroom or gai lan broccoli. These exotic vegetables made the recipes unique, healthy, and scrumptious. You just have to try it for yourself! Altogether this recipe book offers seventy-plus meal ideas from a whole food plant-based diet. As well as being environmentally friendly, the highlights of this book include:

1. A full-color recipe book
2. 70 + healthy meal ideas
3. Gluten-free recipes
4. Healthy vegan recipes
5. Whole grain and legume recipes
6. Raw food recipes
7. Meal preparation made easy

Table of Contents

Preface: My Meal Preparation Experience..............i

Chapter I: Raw Food.................................... 1

1. Arugula, Avocado and Yam Leaves....................4
2. Cucumber, Tomato and Carrot on Spring Mix..............6
3. Mushroom and Pineapple on Mixed Greens...................7
4. Blueberries and Pineapple on Carrot Bed 9
5. Tomato Topped with Enoki Mushrooms 11
6. Blueberries on Shredded Carrots and Arugula 12
7. Sprouted Garbanzo in Zucchini 13
8. Cherry Tomato, Yellow Pepper on Lettuce...................15
9. Walnut and Bean Sprouts 16
10. White Mushrooms on Green Salad...........................17
11. Goji Berries on Mung Bean Sprouts 18
12. Four Easy Dishes of Fresh Living Food 19
13. Raw Food Overpowers Cooked Veggies........................20
14. The Variety of Fresh Fruits 21
   A. Five Fruits: Figs, Papaya, Pineapple, Watermelon and Banana 22
   B. Triple Fruits: Cherries, Green and Red Grapes and Cantaloupe........................23
   C. Delicious Fruit Medley........................24
   D. Seven Fresh Fruits Delight........................25
   E. Two Days' Worth of Fruits 26
   F. It Does Not Last More Than Three Days 27
   G. Fruits as Salad Dressing........................28
15. Unique Scrumptious Raw Combinations
   A. An Energizing Raw Dish 29

B. Surprising Complete Raw Meal 30

16. Short Cut and Quick Fix 31

Chapter II: Whole Grains 33

1. Brown Rice and Black Rice 36
2. Red Quinoa on Brown Rice 37
3. Quinoa Black Rice and Brown Rice 39
4. Farro, Quinoa, Black Rice and Brown Rice 40
5. Lima Beans on Brown Rice 41
6. Soy on Brown Rice..42
7. Red Lentils and Quinoa 43
8. Quinoa, Buckwheat and Red Lentils 44
9. Lentils and Sweet Potato on Quinoa and Brown Rice
    A. Green Lentils and Sweet Potato on Quinoa
        and Brown Rice...46
    B. Red Lentils and Sweet Potato on Quinoa
        and Brown Rice...48
10. Breakfast Oatmeal 49

Chapter III: Beans and Legumes 51

1. Pinto Beans 53
2. Red Kidney Beans and Pinto Beans 54
3. Lentils in Potato 55
4. Tomato and Long Beans on Lentils, Peas and Corn.......56
5. Colorful Mixed Beans 57
6. Taro Root in Garbanzo and Edamame 58
7. Kidney Beans and Green Peas 60
8. The Nutrition of Sprouts 61
9. Delicious Healthy Treats Without White Sugar
    or White Flour 64

Chapter IV: Cooked Vegetable Dishes 66

1. Long Beans and Bitter Melon..71
2. Purple Cauliflower and Broccoli in Tofu......................72
3. Snow Peas, Eggplant and Tofu...................................73
4. Green Beans and Carrots..74
5. Asparagus and Broccoli..75
6. Okra and Red Pepper...76
7. Purple Cauliflower in Long Beans and Snow Peas........78
8. Simply Brussels Sprouts...80
9. Eggplant Tofu 81
10. Asparagus and Peppers in Napa Cabbage......................82
11. Broccoli and Snow Peas Mixed in Tomato..................... 84
12. Okra and Eggplant...85
13. Tricolored Pepper and Broccoli...................................86
14. Broccoli Rabe with Tofu..88
15. Okra, Lotus Root and Black Mushrooms 89
16. Red Pepper in Napa Cabbage 91
17. Green Bok Choy Surrounds Tofu 93
18. Okra on Mixed Veggie Bed...94
19. Shiitake Mushrooms on Kale and Yellow Squash 95
20. Cauliflower Surrounded by Red Pepper and Snow Peas .96
21. Red Pepper and String Beans in Broccoli.....................97
22. Green Bok Choy and Wood Ear Mushrooms 99
23. Asparagus Red Pepper Medley...................................101
24. Okra, Broccoli and Sugar Snap Peas in Tofu Beds........102
25. Red Swiss Chard and Soft Tofu 103
26. Celery, Carrots and Wood Ear Mushrooms 104
27. Brussel Sprouts, Zucchini and Snow Peas 105
28. Broccoli and Tofu on Yellow Carrot Beds 106
29. Red, White and Green Veggie Combo.........................108
30. Triple Green Medley..109

Chapter V: Combination Dishes 110

1. White Beans and Persimmons on Greens 111
2. Tricolored Pepper and Garbanzos on Brown Rice........113
3. Yam Leaves, Papaya, Pecan, Rice and Pinto Beans 115
4. Black Beans, Cherry Tomatoes, Rice and Greens 117
5. Arugula, Avocado, Garbanzo and Kidney Beans
   on Yam Leaves..119

References 121

Yu-Shiaw Chen, Ph.D., CN – Biography 125

My Meal Preparation Experience

I was the second-born in a family of seven children. As a child, I took care of my younger siblings. When I was eight, I started to make dinner for my sister and myself. During most of my childhood, I was Mom's kitchen helper, as she had the huge responsibility of providing meals for eleven family members.

In my career teaching nutrition, I started to host healthy lunch meetings for small groups. And it turned out to be a practical way to teach nutrition. The responses to my homemade lunch meetings were overwhelming. As word got out, the group got bigger and bigger. One time twenty people showed up, and I had to expand to two rooms instantly! All the love and support from the participants kept me going. This recipe book is the result of eighteen years of hosting plant-based healthy lunch meetings.

Did you notice that I don't call it a cook book? Instead, I call it a recipe book, because raw food does not require cooking. In all these years of preparing meals, meal preparation has become second nature to me. It is a part of a healthy lifestyle as well, because it is much healthier to eat at home than to eat out, as you have total control of what you put into your mouth. When you prepare a meal from scratch, you will appreciate how lucky we human beings are to have all this abundant nutrition that nature provides us. If you have the skill to transform raw materials into a delicious dish, that is called culinary art. I am fortunate to have the chance to use this culinary art like a magician. First it is not edible, but when you turn around, it changes into a yummy food. Isn't it wonderful?

As this recipe book is published, I am very grateful to those who have participated in my nutrition programs—especially my lunch meeting participants—all supporting me throughout all these years. This recipe book is the answer to your enthusiastic requests. I would like to thank Mr. John T. Wolfe profusely for your tireless proofreading and valuable feedback. My sincere appreciation goes to Mrs. Kathaleen Donnelly, Mrs. Denise P. DeVito, and Mrs. Vivian Tatem for your continued support and believing in me throughout all these years. There are still countless angels and supporters, who counseled with me and kept referring friends to come to me. I will be forever grateful for all your support.

Certainly, you don't have to be a vegetarian to enjoy this recipe book. However, I hope you will enjoy reading this book and start to make more homemade meals. I hope it gives you some new ideas to try for yourself. I do hope the book motivates you to make the switch and transition to a healthier, whole food, plant-based diet. Thank you very much, and best of luck to you!

Nothing is better than going home to family and eating good food and relaxing. Irina Shayk

Read more at:
https://www.brainyquote.com/quotes/irina_shayk_807961

CHAPTER I
Raw Food

The first step in meal preparation is shopping or gathering materials. To avoid pesticides in produce, I use organic, especially in the Dirty Dozen Plus list. The Environmental Working Group provides lists of produce called the "Dirty Dozen Plus" (highest in pesticides) and the "Clean 15" (lowest in pesticides)**. These are their most recent lists.

Dirty Dozen Plus (highest in pesticides)

Strawberries	Spinach	Nectarines	Apples
Grapes	Peaches	Cherries	Pears
Tomatoes	Celery	Potatoes	Sweet Bell Peppers
Hot Peppers			

Clean Fifteen (lowest in pesticides)

Avocados	GMO Free Sweet Corn	Pineapples	Cabbages
Onions	Sweet Peas Frozen	Papayas	Asparagus
Mangoes	Eggplants	Honeydew Melons	Kiwis
Cantaloupes	Cauliflower	Broccoli	

The Environmental Protection Agency reports that the majority of pesticides now in use are probable or possible cancer causes. Studies of farm workers who work with pesticides suggest a link between pesticide use and brain cancer, Parkinson's disease, multiple myeloma, leukemia, lymphoma, and cancers of the stomach and prostate (ref.1, 2 & 3). These are good reasons to protect our safety and to choose organic produce as much as possible. **https://www.ewg.org/foodnews/full-list.php

Why raw foods in the first place?
Why are raw foods so beneficial?

The reason raw foods are so important in our diet is because of enzymes. The live enzymes in raw foods make a crucial difference in nutrition. Enzymes play a critical role in the body and are involved in an astounding number of metabolic processes. Enzymes are responsible for a variety of bodily processes including: breathing, growth, digestion, producing energy, conducting nerve impulses, clotting blood, recovering after exercise, and balancing the complex processes of the immune system (ref. 4).

Where there is life, there are enzymes. We are alive because enzymes make it possible. Enzymes are the foundation of energy and the life force in all living things (ref. 4). Enzymes are the workforce of the body. They are directly involved in every aspect of bodily functions, including the conception and formation of a human being. Deficiency or exhaustion of the body's enzyme production leads to aging, disease, and death.

We live in a country of abundance, yet most people are enzyme deficient. The most serious threat to the body's supply of endogenous enzymes is the habit of eating cooked and processed foods. Of all the creatures on earth, human beings and their domesticated pets are the only ones that try to live without food enzymes in their diets (ref. 4).

If you eat cooked foods all the time, you are missing very important essential nutrients: live enzymes. That is why this book starts with raw foods. Let me show you how easy it is to prepare raw foods. There are more than twenty recipes in this Chapter 1. They are not scary, so go right ahead, give raw foods a try, and start to enjoy the benefits of live enzymes. Best of luck, and enjoy!

1. Arugula, Avocado and Yam Leaves

INGREDIENTS:

Yam leaves, arugula, watermelon, avocado, enoki mushrooms.

PREPARATION:

- Yam leaves: Remove or peel skin off yam stems. Pick up good yam leaves and soak in water for 10 minutes. Wash them a couple times until water runs clear.
- Arugula: Buy organic or wild arugula prewashed. Rinse in cool water, and spin off excess water and drain.

- Enoki mushrooms: Cut off the root and separate each piece. Wash them in water until water runs clear. Squeeze off the excess water so they are not dripping. Lay them open on the plate. If they are too long, you can cut them in half.
- Watermelon: Cut into inch-long cubes. You can use more or less. Use two cubes of watermelon here in place of salad dressing.
- Avocado: Avocado is a good raw food to supply fat and oil. Together with watermelon, you can have salad without dressing.

This dish introduces you to a very quick and easy way to enjoy an unusual raw recipe. Of course, you can replace yam leaves with romaine lettuce or any other leafy green that you are familiar with.

2. Cucumber, Tomato and Carrot on Spring Mix

INGREDIENTS:

Organic spring mix prewashed salad, organic cherry tomato, organic cucumber, organic carrot slices, sprouted sunflower seeds, organic red pepper slices.

PREPARATION:

Rinse prewashed salad mix with cold water and spin off the excess water. Wash cherry tomatoes and cut the large ones in half. Scrub cucumber and wash it. Slice it into thin slices. Wash red pepper and slice it thin. In a salad bowl, lay down organic spring mix first, then place down the cucumber slices. Add cherry tomatoes and red pepper slices. To finish, add sprouted sunflower seeds. Before you serve, you can spray a few drops of salad dressing.

3. Mushroom and Pineapple on Mixed Greens

INGREDIENTS:

Soaked raw almonds, mushrooms, pineapple cubes, organic spring mix.

PREPARATION:

Prewash and then soak almonds for at least 4 hours beforehand for sprouting. Wash, clean, and spin organic spring green mix. Cleanse and wash mushrooms first, then slice them thin. On a clean plate, place a few layers of spring mix greens, pile mushroom slices on the center of green leaves, add pineapple cubes and sprouted almonds. It is up to you to use salad dressing or not. The pineapple gives you enzymes to enhance digestion and flavor, almonds provide you with protein, and the mushroom slices make a nice combination.

4. Blueberries and Pineapple on Carrot Bed

INGREDIENTS:

Organic carrot, pineapple, and blueberries.

PREPARATION:

Wash and scrub carrot roots carefully and thoroughly. Use a shredder to shred carrots into very fine slices. Soak blueberries for 10 to 20 minutes in cold water and wash them clean. Cut pineapple into cubes. Cover a plate with fine carrot slaw nicely first; then lay down pineapple chunks to cover two-thirds of the carrot bed. Lastly, place the blueberries in the center of the plate. This dish is not just pretty to look at; the combination of these three tastes so good together. Best of all, is the unbeatable nutritional value.

5. Tomato Topped with Enoki Mushrooms

INGREDIENTS:

Enoki mushrooms and tomatoes.

PREPARATION:

Cut the root ends off enoki mushrooms and break each piece to keep them separated. Thoroughly clean and wash them several times. Squeeze water off to let them drain. Wash tomatoes and cut them into wedges. Place tomatoes on a plate and top them with drained enoki mushrooms.

6. Blueberries on Shredded Carrots and Arugula

INGREDIENTS:

Blueberries, organic shredded carrots, arugula leaves, and cantaloupe cubes.

PREPARATION:

Clean and scrub carrots thoroughly. Then shred them with a shredder. Soak blueberries for 10 to 20 minutes in cold water and wash them clean. Wash and spin arugula leaves and place them on the plate. Top the arugula with shredded carrots, cleaned blueberries, and cantaloupe cubes.

7. Sprouted Garbanzo in Zucchini

INGREDIENTS:

Sprouted garbanzo beans and organic zucchini.

PREPARATION:

Wash garbanzo beans a few times, then soak in cold water with more water than just keeping them covered. Beans take in a lot of water in order to wake up and start to germinate. They need at least overnight soaking. In cold weather, they can take a couple days to sprout; make sure you provide adequate fresh water to allow germination. Change the water often to keep it clean.

Wash and scrub the organic zucchini entirely. Cut it to make thin slices. Place zucchini slices around the plate, and put the sprouted garbanzo in the center of the zucchini circle.

8. Cherry Tomato, Yellow Pepper on Lettuce

INGREDIENTS:

Organic spring mix, green leafy vegetables, organic cherry tomatoes, and yellow peppers.

PREPARATION:

Clean organic green and red leafy vegetables a couple times, spin
off excess water and let drain. Wash yellow pepper and slice into
thin slices. Clean and wash cherry tomatoes. In a bowl, put in
spring mix vegetables first. Add a few cherry tomatoes, and lastly
put in yellow pepper slices. You can enjoy it as it is or sprinkle a
few drops of salad dressing.

9. Walnut and Bean Sprouts

INGREDIENTS:

Bean sprouts and walnuts.

PREPARATION:

Soak walnuts in water for a couple hours. Wash bean sprouts twice in cold water. Place clean bean sprouts on a dish, then on the center of the dish load the soaked walnuts. The good part about the walnuts is that among all the tree nuts, walnuts have the highest count of omega 3 oil, an essential fatty acid that we must consume daily.

10. White Mushrooms on Green Salad

INGREDIENTS:

Organic or wild arugula, yam leaves, white mushrooms, shredded carrots, organic red grapes and blueberries.

PREPARATION:

Wash and clean white mushrooms, grapes, blueberries, and arugula. Place arugula on a plate as the first layer, add white mushrooms on top of it, then add grapes and blueberries. Lastly, add shredded carrot on the very top.

11. Goji Berries on Mung Bean Sprouts

INGREDIENTS:

Sprouted mung beans and Goji berries.

PREPARATION:

Wash mung beans several times and soak them in water over-night. Keep in ventilated area to allow sprouting. Change the water when needed. Wash Goji berries and soak briefly. Place sprouted mung beans on a plate, top them with Goji berries and serve.

12. Four Easy Dishes of Fresh Living Food

A. Enoki Mushroom on Leafy Greens

B. Shredded Carrots with Raisins

C. Alfalfa Sprouts and Bean Sprouts

D. Green Lettuce Medley

13. Raw Food Overpowers Cooked Veggies

SIX DISHES WITH HOMEMADE SALAD DRESSING:

A. Alfalfa Sprouts and Goji on Mung Bean Sprouts

B. Fresh Spring Mix/Young Leafy Greens

C. Cherry Tomatoes

D. Sugar Snap Peas

E. Presoaked Mixed Nuts (Almonds, Brazil Nuts, and Pecan)

F. Brussels Sprouts with Mushrooms (the only cooked dish)

G. A Display of Nine Raw Dishes

PREPARATION OF SALAD DRESSING

Mix one teaspoon of organic miso paste in a tablespoon of boiling hot water; smear with a spoon to remove lumps until smooth. Add two tablespoons of apple cider vinegar and one teaspoon of extra virgin olive oil. Blend the mixture with a quarter cup of water. Chill it in refrigerator before serving.

14. The Variety of Fresh Fruits

Fruits are the best type of raw food. Don't forget to include them in your daily intake. In the Healthy Food Plan I presented on page 21 of my book, "***Healthy Eating Wholesome Living***," I explain that it is better to consume at least 20 to 50% of calories from fruits. In other words, we should have five servings of fruits a day. As we are spending so much time and energy preparing vegetables, surprisingly the nutrients you get from fruits are equally vital to our health as those from vegetables.

So what are the nutrients in fruits? Thank you, we finally get to the point. Fruits provide us with abundant nutrition; they have all kinds of vitamins, minerals, live enzymes, antioxidants, phytochemicals, fiber and water. It is God's design, as nature intended for human consumption.

A. Five Fruits: Figs, Papaya, Pineapple, Watermelon and Banana

C. Delicious Fruit Medley

Strawberries, Cherries, Blueberries, Honeydew Melon, Orange and Grapes

D. Seven Fresh Fruits Delight

Raspberries, Tricolored Grapes, Watermelon, Pear, Apple, Orange and Blueberries.

We have never gotten tired of the variety of fruits. The following pictures show our regular daily consumption of fruits.

E. Two Days' Worth of Fruits

Banana, grapes, apple and papaya

F. It Does Not Last More Than Three Days

No, we are not having a party. This photo shows only a week at most supply of fruits for a two-person family. For real, we don't waste our precious food. And you cannot store fruits longer than a week anyway.

G. Fruits as Salad Dressing

Fruits can be a live yummy salad dressing.

INGREDIENTS:

Papaya, shredded carrots, baby spinach and romaine lettuce.

15. Unique Scrumptious Raw Combinations
A. An Energizing Raw Dish

INGREDIENTS:

Avocado, cantaloupe, blueberries, grapes, sprouted pumpkin seeds, carrot slices, red pepper slices, walnuts, pecans, arugula, yam leaves.

B. Surprising Complete Raw Meal

Yam leaves, arugula, cucumber and cherry tomato surround six
fruits, topped with white mushroom and shredded carrots to
make a surprising complete raw meal.

Six fresh fruits are blueberries, red grapes, watermelon, cantaloupe, plum and banana.

16. Short Cut and Quick Fix

AIM Garden Trio

Cocoa Leaf Greens

Fresh fruits and vegetables provide us with vital nutrition, such as vitamins, minerals, live enzymes, antioxidants, phytochemicals, proteins, and fiber. We are supposed to have 5 servings of fruits and 6 servings of vegetables a day. But who has time to do all that shopping, washing, and chopping a daily supply? That's why I'm providing you with this quick fix to rescue, a nutritional supplementation to help you meet the body's demand for more energy. AIM Garden Trio is as close to juicing as possible, with three well-made juice powders. When you mix the powders with water, all their enzymes become active and ready to work for you. Drink it immediately; you will reap the benefits just as you do from juicing fresh produce. I have been blessed with excellent results for the past 25 years.

AIM GardenTrio includes AIM BarleyLife, AIM Just Carrots, and AIM RediBeets. Its wholesome nutrition has generated countless life-changing testimonies (ref. 5). Another whole-food concentrate worth mentioning is Cocoa Leaf Greens, which offers powerful chlorophyll from six plants combined in one jar: barley leaf, spinach leaf, arugula leaf, swiss chard, kale leaf, and broccoli sprouts. These products have revitalized a severe liver cancer patient (ref. 6).

You can order them from http://myaimstore.com/nutrition or any AIM member.

CHAPTER II
Whole Grains

At least 5 to 20% of our calories should come from whole grains, raw nuts, and seeds. Brown rice is unrefined and still contains the bran and germ, which are both removed when processing white rice. Refined white products such as white flour and white rice are not recommended in a healthy diet; because fiber and other important nutrients such as vitamins and minerals are removed during processing (ref. 7).

Brown rice has shown multiple health benefits, including reducing blood pressure (ref. 8), helping you maintain a healthy weight, increasing your potassium, helping your body use insulin effectively, reducing blood vessel damage, and helping control blood sugar. A study found that eating brown rice instead of white rice helped reduce dangerous abdominal fat (ref. 9).

One serving of **black or forbidden rice** contains only around 160 calories, but offers a very high amount of flavonoid phytonutrients, a good source of important fiber, substantial mineral content including iron and copper, and even a good source of plant-based protein. Just the outside hull of the grain has one of the highest levels of anthocyanin antioxidants of any food!

A one-half cup serving of cooked black rice, or about ¼ cup uncooked, contains approximately (in daily recommended values): 160 calories, 1.5 grams of fat, 34 grams of carbohydrates, 2 grams of fiber, 5 grams of protein and 4% DV for iron (ref. 10).

Quinoa is nutrient rich and has significant health benefits, including that it is a complete protein and high in fiber and minerals. For such a tiny seed, quinoa has a lot of protein, 8 grams in one cup cooked. Quinoa is one of the few plant sources of complete protein. This means it contains all nine of the essential amino acids your body needs. Even so, quinoa is higher in calories than other protein sources (ref. 8) and it's gluten-free.

A gluten intolerance is the body's inability to digest or break down the gluten protein found in wheat and certain other grains. Gluten intolerance (also known as gluten sensitivity) can range from a mild sensitivity to gluten to full-blown celiac disease. Common foods that regularly contain ingredients with gluten include: pastas, breads, crackers, seasonings and spice mixes (ref. 11). Almost all the ingredients we use are gluten-free except the ones with notes.

The fact is, **buckwheat** is naturally **gluten-free**. It can be safely eaten and enjoyed by anyone with celiac disease and **gluten** sensitivity. **Buckwheat** is a seed that is not related to **wheat** at all (ref. 12).

Lentils are excellent sources of molybdenum and folate. They are a very good source of dietary fiber, copper, phosphorus, and manganese. Additionally they are a good source of iron, protein, vitamin B1, pantothenic acid, zinc, potassium, and vitamin B6 (ref. 13).

The orange color of the sweet potato comes from an antioxidant called beta-carotene which is converted to vitamin A. Vitamin

A may help restore skin elasticity, promote skin cell turnover, and ultimately contribute to soft, youthful-looking skin. This delicious root vegetable is also a great source of vitamins C and E, both of which may protect our skin from harmful free radicals and keep our complexion radiant (ref. 14).

1. Brown Rice and Black Rice

Raw Brown Rice and Black Rice

Cooked Brown Rice and Black Rice

INGREDIENTS:

Organic brown rice and black rice.

PREPARATION:

Wash 3 cups of organic brown rice three times thoroughly.

Add a quarter cup of black rice and wash two more times. Add 5 cups of filtered water or ***Prill*** ** water and soak for 2 hours. Steam in a rice cooker and cook for 45 minutes. Serve warm and keep it covered at all times.

Prill water is Prill thin water made from Prill's magnesium oxide beads. Prill water is the most unique thin water; it refills dehydrated cells faster. It enhances nutrient absorption and aids in toxin elimination because thin water can more easily enter the cells.

2. Red Quinoa on Brown Rice

INGREDIENTS:

Red organic quinoa and organic brown rice.

PREPARATION:

Wash 3 cups of brown rice a few times.

Add one cup of red quinoa and wash twice. Add 5 and half cups of filtered water or *Prill** water* and soak for 2 hours.

Steam in a covered rice cooker for 45 minutes. Serve warm and keep covered at all times.

Refrigerate the unfinished portion; it is good for the whole week.

3. Quinoa Black Rice and Brown Rice

Raw Quinoa, Black and Brown Rice Mixture

Cooked Quinoa and Brown Rice Mixture

INGREDIENTS:

Organic brown rice, organic black rice, organic quinoa.

PREPARATION:

Wash and soak 5 cups of brown rice for about 2 hours.

Add 2 cups of quinoa, a half cup of black rice, and rinse two more times.

Add 8 cups of filtered water and cook in rice cooker for 50 minutes.

Serve warm and keep covered at all times.

From this point on, the combination of quinoa, black rice, and brown rice will be the foundation of the following several whole grain dishes.

4. Farro, Quinoa, Black Rice and Brown Rice

Raw Farro, Quinoa Black Rice,
and Brown Rice

Cooked Farro Quinoa Black Rice

INGREDIENTS:

Farro, organic brown rice, organic black rice, organic quinoa.

PREPARATION:

Wash and soak 5 cups of brown rice for about 2 hours.

Measure 2 cups of quinoa, half cup of black rice and half cup of farro. Wash them twice, then add to presoaked brown rice.

Add 8 cups of filtered water and cook in rice cooker for 50 minutes.

Serve warm and keep it covered at all times.

5. Lima Beans on Brown Rice

Raw Lima Beans, Quinoa, Black Rice, and Brown Rice

Finished Cooked Lima Beans and Rice Mixture

INGREDIENTS:

Dry lima beans, organic brown rice, organic black rice, organic quinoa.

PREPARATION:

Wash and soak 5 cups of brown rice and a half cup of lima beans for about 2 hours.

Measure 2 cups of quinoa and a half cup of black rice. After rinse them twice, add to presoaked brown rice and lima bean mixture.

6. Soy on Brown Rice

Soy on Brown Rice   Enlarged Soy on Brown Rice

INGREDIENTS:

Organic soy beans, organic brown rice, organic black rice, organic quinoa.

PREPARATION:

Wash and soak one half cup of soy beans for several hours. Then follow the above procedure for preparation of brown rice, quinoa, and black rice. Keep the same ratio, for 5 cups of brown rice, 2 cups of quinoa, a half cup of black rice, add a half cup of soy beans.

Add 2 cups of quinoa, a half cup of black rice, and rinse two more times. Add 9 cups of filtered water or Prill* water and cook in rice cooker for 50 minutes.

Serve warm and keep it covered at all times.

7. Red Lentils and Quinoa

Raw Red Lentils Mixed with Quinoa

Cooked Red Lentils and Quinoa Mixture

INGREDIENTS:

Organic red lentils and organic quinoa.

PREPARATION:

Wash half a cup of red lentils a couple times and soak for at least 2 hours.

Wash 2 cups of quinoa twice and add the presoaked red lentils to it.

Add 4 cups of filtered water and cook in a rice cooker for 40 minutes.

Serve warm or cold. Unfinished portion can be refrigerated and lasts for a few days.

8. Quinoa, Buckwheat and Red Lentils

| Raw Quinoa, Buckwheat, and Red Lentils | Cooked Quinoa, Buckwheat, and Red Lentils |

INGREDIENTS:

Quinoa, buckwheat, and red lentils, all organic.

PREPARATION:

First wash ¼ cup of red lentils a few times and soak in water for at least 2 hours.

Wash 2 cups of quinoa twice, add half cup of buckwheat, and wash again.

Add presoaked red lentils (see picture) and mix together.

Add 5 cups of filtered water or Prill water.

Steam in a covered rice cooker for 30 minutes and simmer for another 15 minutes.

Serve warm or cold and keep it covered at all times.

Refrigerate the unfinished portion; it is good for a few days.

9. Lentils and Sweet Potato on Quinoa and Brown Rice

A. Green Lentils and Sweet Potato on Quinoa and Brown Rice

INGREDIENTS:

Organic green lentils, sweet potato, organic quinoa, and organic brown rice.

PREPARATION:

First wash ¼ cup of green lentils and 3 cups of brown rice a few times and soak in water for at least 2 hours.

Add one cup of quinoa and ¼ cup of black rice and wash twice.

Add 5 and half cups of filtered water or Prill* water.

Add sweet potato cubes to presoaked green lentils and the quinoa and rice mixture.

Steam in a covered rice cooker for 45 minutes.

Serve warm and keep it covered at all times.

Refrigerate the unused portion; it is good for the whole week.

B. Red Lentils and Sweet Potato on Quinoa and Brown Rice

Raw Red Lentils, Sweet Potato on Quinoa and Brown Rice

Cooked Mixture

INGREDIENTS:

Organic red lentils, sweet potato, organic quinoa, and organic brown rice.

PREPARATION:

First add ¼ cup of red lentils to 3 cups of brown rice. Wash the mixture a few times and soak in water for at least 2 hours. Add one cup of quinoa and wash twice more.

Add 5 and half cups of filtered water or Prill water.

Add 1 cup of bite-sized portions of sweet potato.

Cook in rice cooker for 50 minutes.

Serve warm or cold.

10. Breakfast Oatmeal

Prepare 9 Oatmeals

Prepare 12 Oatmeals

Stack up 9 Breakfasts

Oatmeal is not **gluten-free**; however, non-contaminated, pure **oats** are **gluten-free**. They are safe for most people with **gluten** intolerance. The main problem with **oats** in **gluten-free** eating is contamination. Most commercial oats are processed in facilities that also process wheat, barley, and rye (ref. 15).

INGREDIENTS:

Organic rolled oats, black sesame powder, nutritional yeast, soy lecithin, chia seeds, walnuts, pecans, sprouted sunflower seeds, almond slices, and Goji berries. Not shown in the pictures: organic raisins or cranberries and dates. Organic flax meal and organic unfiltered flaxseed oil.

PREPARATION:

This is a quick way to make your almost instant nutritious breakfast, as it is the most important meal of the day. So I do prepare it ahead of time, usually on the weekend. All of above ingredients were pre-measured and put together ahead of time, as the above picture showing 9 breakfasts. Each morning, you only need to pour boiling hot water into the bowl and cover it for 5 minutes. To ensure you get sufficient essential fatty acids, right before you eat, it is good to add organic flaxseed meal and a tablespoon of unfiltered flaxseed oil into the oatmeal mixture. It makes a complete nutritious and also scrumptious warm breakfast instantly.

You may choose to use empty plastic containers with a lid, which are easy to store and stack them up nicely as the above pictures. There is additional breakfast recipe on page 29 through 31 of my book "*Healthy Eating Wholesome Living*".

CHAPTER III
Beans and Legumes

Legumes — a class of vegetables that includes beans, peas, and lentils — are among the most versatile and nutritious foods available (ref. 16). Legumes are typically low in fat, and high in folate, potassium, iron, and magnesium. They also contain beneficial fats and soluble and insoluble fiber. A good source of protein, legumes can be a healthy substitute for meat, which has more fat and cholesterol.

Beans and legumes have a number of health benefits, including reducing cholesterol, decreasing blood sugar levels, and increasing healthy gut bacteria (ref. 17).

For instance, a study showed that pinto beans may reduce LDL cholesterol as well as increase the production of propionate, a short-chain fatty acid produced by gut bacteria. Propionate is good for gut health. Like many other beans, pinto beans can also reduce the rise in blood sugar that happens after eating a meal (ref. 18).

There are a wide variety of dry beans available in the supermarket. All dry beans require soaking in water to rehydrate them for quicker cooking. Even though it takes time, I feel better to start from scratch soaking dry organic beans. However, if you don't like to soak dry beans, you may use canned beans instead. You need to read the label carefully; use only the cans that have all the ingredients organic and make sure they contain no preservatives or chemicals.

Planning ahead is the key to handle the kitchen work and to avoid stress. Using the following procedure, you can make a large batch of any beans or more than one type of legumes, store portions in the freezer and some in refrigerator, which can help you to make a healthy meal instantly. When you have prepared whole grain and legume dishes ahead of time, then more than half of dinner is ready. All you have to do is wash your salad and veggies and add some fresh fruits to have a complete meal quickly.

1. Pinto Beans

Soaked Pinto Beans   Added Kelp and Star Aniseed Herb for flavoring

Wash pinto beans several times and soak them with two volumes of water at room temperature for half a day or overnight (at least 5 hours) or until beans begin to open up. Replace the water with filtered water or Prill** water and cook in a rice cooker for about 50 minutes to an hour. You may use any stainless steel pot or a steamer, but you need to watch out and keep adding water. To speed up the cooking, you may add kelp to help soften the beans. During the cooking, I like to add star aniseed herb for a nice seasoning. After cooking, add a dash of sea salt for flavoring. Beans made this way will last for several days in the refrigerator. You can keep them in the freezer for longer storage, too.

Prill water is Prill thin water made from Prill's magnesium oxide beads. Prill water is the most unique thin water; it refills dehydrated cells faster. It enhances nutrient absorption and aids in toxin elimination because thin water can more easily enter the cells.

2. Red Kidney Beans and Pinto Beans

It's nice to mix more than one kind of beans together. Red kidney beans go well with pinto beans, because of their similarity. Prepare both red kidney beans and pinto beans exactly the same way as the above procedure. Just like the color, they complement each other in taste, too.

3. Lentils in Potato

Wash green lentils thoroughly and soak them in room temperature water for a couple hours. Scrub the organic potato skin very well. After washing and cleaning, cut it into small bite-sized pieces. In a large pot boil three times of their volumes of water, add both soaked lentils and cut potato cubes and keep boiling for about 15 minutes or until lentils open up. Add a dash of sea salt for taste and smear one to two teaspoons of organic miso paste into the soup. It makes a delicious, warm, hearty soup.

4. Tomato and Long Beans on Lentils, Peas and Corn

Wash green lentils thoroughly and soak them in water for two hours before cooking. Wash organic tomatoes, carrots, long beans, and cut them into bite-sized pieces. Wash peas and corn as well. In a stainless steel pan, boil carrots and lentils in two times of their volumes of water for about 10 minutes. Add two teaspoons of oil together with long beans, cut corn, and tomatoes and cook another 2 minutes with cover. Then add green peas with a dash of sea salt and black pepper if you like. Mix well and stir fry briefly; serve warm.

5. Colorful Mixed Beans

Prepare the black beans, using the same procedure for pinto beans, ahead of time. Wash and cut carrots into small cubes. Rinse a block of organic tofu and cut to small cubes as well. Clean mushrooms and red peppers and slice them thin. Simmer sliced ginger in water and 1 teaspoon of olive oil in a stainless steel pot. First add carrot cubes, tofu, and red pepper to cook for two minutes, then add the cooked black beans, edamame, corn and mushroom slices to pot. Mix well and stir fry quickly. Add a dash of sea salt and /or black pepper to taste.

6. Taro Root in Garbanzo and Edamame

Follow the same procedure as in pinto beans preparation to prepare organic garbanzo beans. First wash clean and soak garbanzos in three volumes of water overnight until chickpeas start to germinate. Then cook them the same way as pinto beans, for 50 minutes. After seasoning, you can store them in the refrigerator or freezer for later use.

Wash and clean taro root thoroughly and cut it into small bite-sized cubes. Simmer sliced ginger in water and 1 teaspoon of olive oil in a stainless steel pot. Add taro root pieces to cook for 2 minutes, then add the prepared garbanzo and organic edamame beans to pot. Quickly stir fry and mix well. Add a dash of sea salt and black pepper for seasoning. You may use any desired flavoring, as you wish.

7. Kidney Beans and Green Peas

Follow the previous bean procedure to prepare kidney beans ahead of time. Wash and cut carrots into small cubes. In a stainless steel pan, boil carrots slices in water for about 5 minutes. Add prepared kidney beans, green peas and corn, mix well, and stir fry quickly. Add a dash of sea salt and black pepper or any other flavoring for seasoning. Serve warm or cold.

8. The Nutrition of Sprouts

Sprouting Lentils

Mung Bean Sprouts

Sprouted Chickpeas and Walnuts

Sprouted Almonds in Squash

The simple process of **sprouting** brings out many enzymes in germinated seeds, legumes, and grains, making them easier to digest. It also increases the amounts and bioavailability of protein, vitamins, and minerals, transforming them into **nutrition powerhouses** (ref. 16). Sprouts contain notable amounts of vitamin C; traces of B vitamins; a surprising amount of protein and fiber; and small amounts of calcium, iron, magnesium, phosphorus, potassium and zinc. In particular, mung beans are quite high in potassium, with 155 mg in a cup-size serving (ref. 17). Another **benefit**: because the germinating process breaks down some of the starchy endosperm, **sprouted** grains may have less starch and be easier to digest than regular grains (ref. 18).

So many sprouts are available in the supermarket. However, it is easy to sprout them at home. I usually soak beans anyway. Longer soaking allows them to sprout. You can stop them any time by cooking or eating them. The best part of nutrition is to eat the raw sprouts as shown in the above pictures: sprouting lentils, garbanzo and mung bean sprouts. They are among my commonly served raw dishes. They are scrumptious, nutritious and easy to make. The soaking time varies. It can take from half a day to over two to three nights. You need to change water often and watch out. Basically, they need water, air, and sunlight. They germinate faster on a sunny day than a rainy day.

If eating fresh raw sprouts does not appeal to you, I have recommended a homemade vegetable dip for you to try to add on any sprouts or salad.

A. Sprouted Almond Surrounded by Yellow Squash

INGREDIENTS:

Sprouted almonds and yellow squash.

PREPARATION:

Wash almonds a couple times and soak them in cold water for at least 4 hours. Clean and scrub the organic yellow squash thoroughly. Then slice it into thin slices. Place the yellow squash slices around a plate in a circle; inside the circle fill up with sprouted almonds.

B. Recommended Vegetable Dip

Start with 1 tablespoon of organic Miso soybean paste, add 1 tablespoon of vinegar and mix well. Add half a box of Silken Soy tofu (soft tofu) and 1 teaspoon of AIM Just Carrots powder and mix well. Place in refrigerator 30 minutes prior to serving.

9. Delicious Healthy Treats Without White Sugar or White Flour

You can make many different desserts out of this preparation. Adzuki beans and mung beans are the most commonly used legumes. Let's take adzuki as an example first.

A. Adzuki Bean (Red Bean) Soup

Wash a few times one cup of organic adzuki beans, then soak in room temperature water overnight. It may take more than one night's soaking (depends on the season) until beans starts to germinate. The beans, after they rehydrate, will swell and open up. Replace water with three cups of filtered water; add some dry cranberries as the seasoning, and cook for around 50 minutes. When the beans turn soft and mushy, that it is the yummy adzuki bean soup for your treat. If they are not soft yet, add more water and cook some more or until beans become soft.

B. Mung Bean (Green Bean) Soup

Follow the above protocol with a cup of organic mung beans. The soaking time will be reduced as mung beans are smaller and easier to get rehydrated. Both mung bean soup and adzuki soup are popular treats in Asian families.

For making bean soups as a treat, in addition to dried cranberries, there are numerous dried fruits available for your consideration: organic raisins, organic dates, organic figs, dried blueberries, dried cherries, plums, apricots, mango, pineapple cubes, dried papaya cubes… you name it. If it is not enough, I frequently use sweet potato as a treat. See the following picture of hearty mung bean treat. The way to make it is to first cook soaked mung beans with cranberries and organic raisins for half an hour, and then add sweet potato cubes to cook for additional 10 minutes. It is that easy to have a yummy, authentic treat!

Sprouting Mung Beans

Adzuki Beans (Soaked 15 Hours)

Add Dry Cranberries

Cooked Adzuki Soup

Mung Bean Raisin Soup

Hearty Mung Bean Treat

CHAPTER IV
Cooked Vegetable Dishes

Before I present any cooked dishes, let me introduce you to a few exotic ingredients or unfamiliar vegetables, which I commonly use in my cooking, as they are among my favorites.

Bitter melon: Since this insulin-like activity may help protect against insulin resistance and keep your blood sugar from rising, it's thought that **bitter melon may help fight diabetes**. In addition, bitter melon is said to help treat and/or prevent health problems such as acne, constipation and more (ref. 19).

Bitter Melon

Okra

Okra: Okra's high levels of **vitamin A**, **B vitamins** (B1, B2, B6), **vitamin C** and traces of **zinc** and **calcium**, make it an ideal vegetable to eat during **pregnancy**. Okra also serves as a supplement for **fiber** and **folic acid**. This helps prevent birth defects like spina bifida and can even stop constipation during pregnancy (ref. 20).

A protein in okra, called **lectin**, is also found in peanuts and beans. In one study, researchers extracted lectin from okra to test on breast cancer cells and found the cancer growth to not only decrease by 63%, but to kill 72% of the cancer cells (ref. 21).

Shiitake Mushrooms: Shiitake can fight tumors. These flavorful, meaty mushrooms contain lentinan, which is a natural anti-tumor compound. It has been developed by the Japanese into a beneficial anti-cancer treatment. In turn, it is an excellent source of vitamin D, and helps fight infections. Four to five ounces per day is recommended (ref. 22).

Fresh Shiitake Mushroom

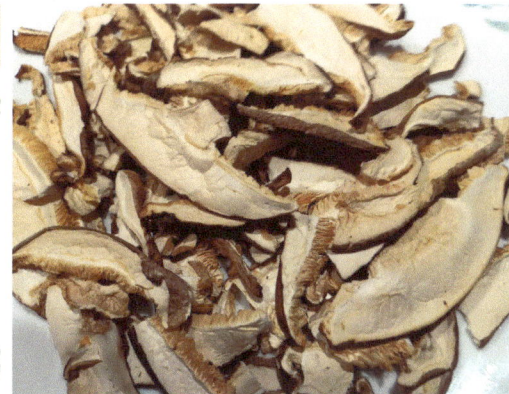

Dried Shiitake Mushroom

Lotus Root: Crunchy, delicately flavored lotus root is an edible rhizome (root) of the lotus plant. Almost all the parts of the plant—root, young flower stalks, and seeds—are employed in cuisine. For centuries, lotus plant and its parts have been held in high esteem in far East societies, especially in the Chinese and Japanese cultures (ref. 23).

The health benefits of lotus root can be attributed to its unique mix of vitamins, minerals, and phytonutrients, including potassium, phosphorous, copper, iron, and manganese, as well as thiamin, pantothenic acid, zinc, vitamin B6, and vitamin C. It is also a very significant source of dietary fiber and a decent source of protein (ref. 24). The health benefits of lotus root include:

Boosts immunity and aids in weight management; helps improve health of skin, hair, and eyes; gives relief from headaches and stress; stimulates blood circulation; facilitates digestion and bowel movements.

Lotus Root   Wood Ear Mushrooms

Wood Ear Mushrooms (also known as black fungus mushrooms):

With their thin, gray-brown to black color and rubbery texture, wood ear mushrooms have a high dietary fiber content and are high in iron, and in free-radical-busting vitamin B-2 (ref. 25), as well as cellulose and a special plant collagen (ref. 24).

The health benefits of black fungus mushrooms include: reduce the risk of cardiovascular disorders, have the ability to prevent Alzheimer's disorders, prevent irritation and inflammation.

Wood ear mushrooms contain vitamin K, which can assist in prevention of blood coagulation, thrombosis, and embolism, help lower cholesterol, prevent anemia, and reduce the risk of stress. And it can be an antidote to free radicals (ref. 27).

Gai-Lan (also known as Chinese broccoli):
Gai-lan is a good source of vitamin E (alpha-tocopherol), vitamin B6, iron, phosphorus, zinc, and copper, and a very good source of dietary fiber, vitamin A, vitamin C, vitamin K, thiamin, riboflavin, folate, calcium, magnesium, potassium, and manganese (ref. 28).

Chinese broccoli, or gai-lan, is a nutritious green leafy vegetable and a member of the Brassica family of vegetables. Gai-lan broccoli is commonly used in Chinese cuisine. Its potential health benefits include protection against cancer, cardiovascular benefits, asthma relief, and improved eye health (ref. 29).

Gai-Lan

Turmeric—and especially its most active compound, curcumin—have many scientifically proven health benefits, such as the potential to prevent heart disease, Alzheimer's, and **cancer**. It's a potent **anti-inflammatory** and **antioxidant** and may also help improve symptoms of **depression** and **arthritis** (ref. 30).

Cooked Vegetable Dishes
1. Long Beans and Bitter Melon

Wash, clean, and cut bitter melon, carrot and long beans. Wash and rinse bean sprouts and wood ear mushrooms. Slice mushrooms. Heat up 3 tablespoons of water with carrot slices first.

Add long beans, bitter melon and 1 teaspoon of oil and cook with cover on for 1 minute or until hot. Add wood ear mushrooms and bean sprouts and cook half a minute. Add sea salt to taste and serve warm.

2. Purple Cauliflower and Broccoli in Tofu

Wash and cut purple cauliflower and broccoli into bite-sized pieces. Simmer sliced ginger in water and 1 teaspoon of olive oil to stainless steel pot. Cut 1 box of organic tofu (firm tofu) into bite-sized cubes and add to pot. Then add broccoli, purple cauliflower and sliced mushrooms, cook until broccoli turns bright green. Add a dash of sea salt to taste, then mix and serve. Optionally season with spices such as turmeric or black pepper as desired.

3. Snow Peas, Eggplant and Tofu

Wash and slice eggplant into bite-sized pieces. Clean and wash snow peas. Simmer sliced ginger in water and 1 teaspoon of olive oil to stainless steel pot. Cut 1 box of organic tofu (firm tofu) into bite-sized cubes and add to pot. Add eggplant slices into the pot and cook half a minute or until eggplant turn soft. Add snow peas and a dash of sea salt to taste, mix and heat briefly until the snow peas turn brilliant green. Transfer to a plate and serve.

4. Green Beans and Carrots

Clean yellow and orange colored carrots, and cut into thin slices. Wash green beans and break into bite-sized segments, about 2 inches long. Heat stainless steel pot at a high temperature with some water. Add carrot slices and cook in water first for a minute. Then add sliced fresh ginger, 1 teaspoon of olive oil, and green beans to pot. Cover pot to steam vegetables (slightly tender) or until green beans turn bright green. Season with a dash of sea salt and optional black pepper to taste. Stir fry slightly and serve warm or cold.

5. Asparagus and Broccoli

Clean, rinse and cut asparagus, broccoli, carrots, yellow squash, and mushrooms. Heat stainless steel pot at a high temperature with some water; add sliced fresh ginger, carrots, and 1 teaspoon of olive oil and cook for a minute. Then add sliced yellow squash and broccoli, stir fry for half a minute. Lastly add asparagus, cover pot to steam vegetables briefly or until asparagus turn bright green. Add sliced mushrooms and a dash of sea salt to taste. Stir fry slightly and serve warm or cold.

6. Okra and Red Pepper

Wash, clean and cut red pepper, okra, dry tofu and mushrooms.

Heat stainless steel pot with water at a high temperature,

Add sliced ginger, red pepper, and 1 teaspoon olive oil or filtered coconut oil.

Cover the pot and cook briefly, then add dry tofu and okra slices to pot.

Heat for a minute or until okra turns bright green. Add sliced mushrooms and stir fry.

Season with sea salt to taste or any desired flavor and serve.

7. Purple Cauliflower in Long Beans and Snow Peas

Clean, wash and soak purple cauliflower, long beans and snow peas.

Heat a few drops of water in a stainless steel pot at a high temperature.

Add first sliced ginger, purple cauliflower, then long beans & 1 teaspoon of olive oil to pot.

Cover pot to steam vegetables to slightly tender, about 1 minute.

Add rinsed sliced mushrooms, snow peas, and a pinch of sea salt.

Stir, mix and cover pot for another half a minute or until snow peas turn bright green.

Serve warm or cold.

8. Simply Brussels Sprouts

Wash and clean brussels sprouts and slice each one into 3 slices.

Add 2 tablespoons of water and half a teaspoon of oil to pot.

Heat pot to a high temperature and add sliced brussels sprouts.

Simmer it for one to 2 minutes or until color turns bright green.

Add sliced mushrooms and cover the pot briefly.

Stir fry, add sea salt to taste, and serve.

9. Eggplant Tofu

Wash and slice eggplant into bite-sized pieces. Simmer sliced ginger in water and 1 teaspoon of olive oil to stainless steel pot. Cut 1 box of organic tofu (firm tofu) into bite-sized cubes and add to pot.

Add eggplant slices into the pot and cook half a minute or until eggplant turns soft.

Add a dash of sea salt to taste, mix and serve.

10. Asparagus and Peppers in Napa Cabbage

Wash and soak napa cabbage, then cut into bite-sized portions.

Clean and slice asparagus and orange peppers. Soak black mushrooms and slice them.

Simmer sliced ginger in water and 1 teaspoon of olive oil to stainless steel pot.

Add sliced black mushrooms and napa cabbage and cook for a minute or two.

Add peppers and asparagus, and heat another minute or until asparagus turns bright green.

Add a dash of sea salt or any desired flavoring to taste, mix, and serve.

11. Broccoli and Snow Peas Mixed in Tomato

Wash and cut broccoli and tomato. Clean snow peas.

Simmer sliced ginger in water and add 1 teaspoon of olive oil to stainless steel pot.

Add broccoli and cook for a minute. Then add snow peas and tomato to pot.

Stir fry briefly until snow peas turn bright green. Season with a dash of sea salt and serve.

12. Okra and Eggplant

Wash clean and cut eggplant and okra. Simmer sliced ginger in water and 1 teaspoon of olive oil to stainless steel pan. You may use coconut oil instead of olive oil if you prefer.

First add eggplant and cook briefly for half a minute. Then add okra and quick stir mix on the hot pan for half a minute or until okra turns color. Season with sea salt to taste or any desired flavor and serve.

13. Tricolored Pepper and Broccoli

Wash and cut broccoli into bite-sized portion. Clean and slice yellow, orange, and red peppers.

Also rinse and cut 1 box of organic tofu (firm tofu) into bite-sized cubes.

Simmer sliced ginger in water and 1 teaspoon of olive oil to stainless steel pot.

First add tofu to pot and then add yellow, orange, and red pepper slices to pot. It is optional to add sliced mushrooms or wood ear mushrooms.

Cook briefly and add broccoli into the pot and cook half a minute or until broccoli turns green.

Add a dash of sea salt to taste, mix well, and serve.

14. Broccoli Rabe with Tofu

Wash clean broccoli rabe a few times and cut into inch-long pieces.

Rinse and cut 1 box of organic tofu (firm tofu) into bite-sized cubes.

Simmer sliced ginger in water and 1 teaspoon of coconut oil to stainless steel pot.

Add tofu first to pot and cook briefly or for half a minute.

Then add broccoli rabe and a dash of sea salt; quickly stir fry. Mix well and serve warm.

15. Okra, Lotus Root and Black Mushrooms

Clean and soak black mushrooms in water for about 20 minutes. Slice them thin.

Wash clean and slice lotus root, yellow squash, and okra.

Simmer sliced ginger in water and 1 teaspoon of coconut oil to stainless steel pot.

Add black mushroom first, then lotus root, yellow squash, and cook briefly or for half a minute.

Then add okra and a dash of sea salt, quickly stir fry until okra turns green. Mix well and serve warm.

16. Red Pepper in Napa Cabbage

Clean and soak black mushrooms in water for about 20 minutes. Slice them thin.

Wash clean red pepper and napa cabbage, and cut them into bite-sized pieces.

Simmer sliced ginger in water and 1 teaspoon of coconut oil to stainless steel pot.

Add black mushroom first, then napa cabbage and cook for a minute.

Then add red pepper and a dash of sea salt and cook another minute.

Quickly stir fry, mix well, and serve warm.

17. Green Bok Choy Surrounds Tofu

Scrub and clean sweet potatoes thoroughly. Slice them into pieces a quarter-inch thick and steam in a rice cooker for 5 minutes. Wash and clean green bok choy. Soak some Goji berries in water. Also rinse and cut 1 box of organic soft tofu into bite-sized cubes. Stir fry tofu in 1 teaspoon of coconut oil in stainless steel pot. Add a dash of sea salt, Goji berries, and steamed sweet potato slices and mix well. In boiling water, add green bok choy and a dash of sea salt to cook very briefly or until it turns bright green color. Drain and arrange vegetables around tofu on a plate.

18. Okra on Mixed Veggie Bed

Wash clean and cut carrots, cauliflower, and okra. Clean mushrooms and slice them thin.

Rinse dry tofu and cut into thin slices. Simmer two tablespoons of water with carrot slices and cauliflower in a stainless steel pan to cook for a minute. Add 1 teaspoon of coconut oil, a dash of sea salt and dry tofu slices to the pan. Lastly add okra and mushroom slices and cook with the cover on briefly or until okra turns bright green color. Mix well and try the taste. You may add black pepper or turmeric or both, or other seasonings for extra flavor. Serve warm.

19. Shiitake Mushrooms on Kale and Yellow Squash

Scrub wash and cut yellow squash into slices. Clean kale leaves, remove unwanted parts, and cut into pieces one to two inches long. Wash fresh shiitake mushrooms and slice them into thin slices. Simmer ginger slices in water with 1 teaspoon of coconut oil to a stainless steel pan. Add yellow squash slices, cut kale, and shiitake mushroom slices and cook very briefly for half a minute or until kale turns bright green. Add a dash of sea salt or any desired flavoring to taste, mix, and serve warm.

20. Cauliflower Surrounded by Red Pepper and Snow Peas

Wash, clean, and cut cauliflower and red pepper into bite-sized pieces. String and wash snow peas.

Clean mushrooms and cut them to thin slices. Slice pre-seasoned fried organic tofu into thin slices. In a stainless steel pan, simmer ginger slices in water with 1 teaspoon of coconut oil. Add cauliflower and red pepper to cook shortly. Then add tofu, mushroom slices, and snow peas and cook for half a minute or until snow peas turn bright color. Add a dash of sea salt or any desired flavoring to taste, mix, and serve warm.

21. Red Pepper and String Beans in Broccoli

Scrub white carrot, clean, and cut into thin slices. Wash and cut red pepper and broccoli into bite-sized pieces. String the string beans, wash, and cut into 2-inch-long pieces. Wash and slice mushrooms. In a stainless steel pan, simmer ginger slices in water with 1 teaspoon of coconut oil. Add white carrot and red pepper first to cook briefly. Then add string beans, broccoli, mushrooms, and sea salt to cook for half a minute or until broccoli turn bright color. Mix well and try the taste. You may add black pepper or turmeric or both, or other seasoning for extra flavor. Serve warm.

22. Green Bok Choy and Wood Ear Mushrooms

Clean and wash bok choy, wood ear mushrooms, and mushrooms several times to remove the dirt and debris. Cut bok choy and both mushrooms into bite-sized portions. Heat stainless steel pot with water at a high temperature; add sliced ginger and 1 teaspoon olive oil or filtered coconut oil. Add bok choy and wood ear mushrooms to pot. Cover pot to steam vegetables (slightly tender) and simmer for half a minute. Add sliced mushrooms and sea salt to taste and/ or other seasoning. Serve warm or cold.

23. Asparagus Red Pepper Medley

String asparagus, wash and cut into 2-inch-long pieces. Wash and cut red pepper to slices. Cleanse thick dry tofu and cut into thin slices. Rinse shredded white tofu. Simmer ginger slices in water with 1 teaspoon of coconut oil in a stainless steel pan. Add red pepper, thick dry tofu slices, shredded tofu, asparagus, and a dash of sea salt and stir fry for a minute. You may add turmeric or black pepper or both or other seasoning for extra flavor. Serve warm.

24. Okra, Broccoli and Sugar Snap Peas in Tofu Beds

String and wash sugar snap peas. Wash and cut broccoli and okra. Cut broccoli into bite-sized pieces and slice each okra into 2 or 3 slices. Wash and cut mushrooms and wood ear mushrooms into slices. Rinse and cut 1 box of organic soft tofu into bite-sized cubes. In a stainless steel pan, simmer ginger slices in water with 1 teaspoon of coconut oil. First add tofu, then broccoli and wood ear mushrooms; cook briefly. Then add okra, sugar snap peas, and mushrooms in the end. Stir fry on high heat quickly until peas turn bright green. Add a dash of sea salt and black pepper (optional) to taste. Serve warm.

25. Red Swiss Chard and Soft Tofu

Soak and wash red Swiss chard and cut into bite-sized pieces. Rinse and cut 1 box of organic soft tofu into bite-sized cubes. In a stainless steel pan, simmer ginger slices in water with 1 teaspoon of coconut oil (or olive oil). Add soft tofu and cook for half a minute; then add red Swiss chard to pan and cook another half a minute or until Swiss chard turns bright color. Add a dash of sea salt and turmeric (optional) to taste. Serve warm.

26. Celery, Carrots and Wood Ear Mushrooms

Scrub carrots and wash thoroughly; cut into thin slices. Soak wood ear mushrooms and cut into slices. Wash and slice celery into thin slices. Simmer carrot slices in water with 1 teaspoon of coconut oil (or olive oil) in a stainless steel pan. Add celery slices and wood ear mushrooms and cook for half a minute or until celery turns green. Add a dash of sea salt to taste. You may add any seasoning as you like. Serve warm.

27. Brussel Sprouts, Zucchini and Snow Peas

Wash clean and cut zucchini and brussels sprouts into thin slices. String and wash snow peas. In a stainless steel pan, simmer sliced ginger in water with 1 teaspoon of coconut oil; add brussels sprouts, zucchini slices, and the last snow peas. Cook very briefly or until snow peas turn bright green. Add a dash of sea salt to taste and any desired flavoring. Mix well and serve warm.

28. Broccoli and Tofu on Yellow Carrot Beds

Scrub yellow carrot, wash and cut into thin slices. Wash clean and cut broccoli and eggplant into bite-sized pieces.

Wash and slice mushrooms into slices. Rinse and cut 1 box of organic soft tofu into bite-sized cubes. Simmer sliced ginger in water with 1 teaspoon of coconut oil in a stainless steel pan. Add yellow carrot slices and cook first for a minute, add tofu, eggplant slices and broccoli, then mushroom slices at the end. Stir fry briefly or cook until broccoli turns bright green. Add a dash of sea salt and turmeric (optional) to taste. Serve warm.

29. Red, White and Green Veggie Combo

Wash and cut collard greens, red pepper, and tofu into small pieces. Start with a few drops of water and oil in pot, add diced tofu and red pepper. Simmer for a minute and add cut collard greens and edamame beans. Stir fry quickly, add sea salt to taste.

30. Triple Green Medley

Wash and cut gai-lan, zucchini, and okra. Start with a few drops of water and oil in pot; add gai-lan, zucchini, and okra.

Stir fry each individual vegetable separately for a minute or until vegetables turn bright green.

Add sea salt to taste. Arrange on a plate nicely. Or you may mix them well and serve warm.

CHAPTER V
Combination Dishes

In this Chapter I have combined raw vegetables, fresh fruits, and raw nuts with cooked legumes, whole grains, and stir-fried veggies, all in one dish. So you get your live enzymes in raw foods and all the balanced nutrition in one plate.

About Chinese Water Spinach

Chinese water spinach is a long, leafy green vegetable with hollow stems that is grown in water- or damp soil. It also goes by the name of ong choy in Cantonese or kōng xīn cài (空心菜) in Mandarin, which translates to "hollow heart vegetable" (ref. 31).

1. White Beans and Persimmons on Greens

INGREDIENTS:

Organic red leaf lettuce, organic romaine lettuce and other green leafy vegetables, organic red pepper, organic cherry tomatoes, persimmons, and (the only cooked ingredient) organic white beans

PREPARATION:

Ahead of time, presoak organic white beans overnight. Cook them as described in Chapter III and store them in the refrigerator. Wash and clean all vegetables several times and spin in a spinner to remove excessive water. Clean red pepper and slice it into thin slices. Also slice persimmons into thin wedges after washing them. On a plate, lay down green leafy vegetables and red lettuce first, then red pepper, cherry tomatoes, and persimmon wedges. At last, on top of the center green leaves, place precooked white beans. Then your plate of rainbow-colored nutrition is ready for you!

2. Tricolored Pepper and Garbanzos on Brown Rice

INGREDIENTS:

Organic tricolored peppers, organic spring mix vegetables, organic broccoli, organic yellow squash, organic celery, organic brown rice, organic garbanzo beans, ginger slices.

PREPARATION:

Ahead of time presoak, and cook organic garbanzo beans as described in Chapter III. Make organic brown rice in rice cooker as described in Chapter II. Wash and clean all the vegetables a few times. Cut tricolored pepper and yellow squash into slices. Cut broccoli into bite-sized cubes and celery into even smaller dices. Simmer sliced ginger in water and 1 teaspoon of olive oil in a stainless steel pot. Add celery dices, precooked garbanzo beans and brown rice, mix well and stir fry quickly. Add sea salt and black pepper to taste. On a plate lay down fresh leafy greens, tricolored peppers, yellow squash slices, and broccoli cubes. On the side, put the garbanzo and brown rice mixture to make a complete colorful meal.

3. Yam Leaves, Papaya, Pecan, Rice and Pinto Beans

INGREDIENTS:

Organic lettuce, organic pecans, organic pinto beans, organic brown rice and black rice, farro, organic broccoli, yam leaves, bok choy, and papaya.

PREPARATION:

Precook pinto beans as stated on page 53 of Chapter III. Precook brown rice, black rice and farro as described on page 40 of Chapter II. Wash all the vegetables and papaya. Cut

lettuce, and yam leaves cut into tiny strips. Cut papaya into large chunks. Soak pecans for an hour in water. Throw cut broccoli cubes and bok choy into a pot with water boiling, quickly boil for half a minute and drain quickly. On a plate lay down yam strips, papaya cubes, lettuce pieces, and soaked pecans. On the other side, lay down the cooked mixture of farro, brown rice and black rice, broccoli, bok choy, and pinto beans. That is a combination of live food and cooked food to enjoy.

4. Black Beans, Cherry Tomatoes, Rice and Greens

INGREDIENTS:

Organic brown rice, organic black beans, organic cherry to-matoes, organic celery, Chinese water spinach, mushrooms, spaghetti squash, ginger.

PREPARATION:

Ahead of time, presoak and cook black beans as the procedure on page 53 of Chapter III. Cook brown rice in a rice cooker as stated on page 36 of Chapter II.

Cut spaghetti squash in half lengthwise. Scrape out and discard seeds and membranes. Bake in a preheated oven at 350°F for 45 to 50 minutes or until tender (ref. 32).

Wash all the vegetables thoroughly. Cut the Chinese water spinach into 1-inch-wide pieces. Chop celery into half-inch discs. Slice mushroom into thin slices. Simmer sliced ginger in water and 1 teaspoon of coconut oil in a stainless steel pot. Add celery discs and mushroom slices, and stir fry quickly. Add a dash of sea salt and black pepper for taste.

On the side of a plate, place baked spaghetti squash, cooked black beans, raw Chinese water spinach, and cherry tomatoes. In the center of the plate, first put brown rice down, then on top of it layer the stir-fried celery and mushrooms on rice. It is a good combination of brown rice with raw and cooked veggies, plus black beans to make a complete, satisfactory meal.

5. Arugula, Avocado, Garbanzo and Kidney Beans on Yam Leaves

INGREDIENTS:

Yam leaves, arugula, watermelon, avocado, enoki mushrooms, organic garbanzo and organic red kidney beans.

PREPARATION:

Presoak in water then cook both garbanzo and red kidney beans, following the procedure on page 54 of Chapter III.

Wash clean all the vegetables and repeat the whole preparation on page 4-5 of Chapter I. After preparing the whole plate of raw vegetables, avocado, enoki mushrooms, and watermelon, add the cooked garbanzo and red kidney beans. That is a nice raw overpowering cooked food dish. You get all the goodness of balanced nutrition without spending a whole lot of time working in the kitchen.

References

Preface

1. Brown TP, Rumsby PC, Capleton AC, et al: Pesticides and Parkinson's disease--is there a link? Environ Health Perspect 2006, 114:156-164.

2. Sanderson WT, Talaska G, Zaebst D, et al: Pesticide prioritization for a brain cancer case-control study. Environ Res 1997, 74:133-144.

3. Zahm SH, Blair A: Cancer among migrant and seasonal farmworkers: an epidemiologic review and research agenda. Am J Ind Med 1993, 24:753-766.

Chapter 1

4. https://sciencebasedmedicine.org/systemic-enzyme-therapy/

5. Pages 44-48, "Healthy Eating Wholesome Living" by Yu-Shiaw Chen, Ph.D., 2011, www.linutrition.com

6. Pages 34-44, "Healthy Eating Wholesome Living" by Yu-Shiaw Chen, Ph.D., 2011, www.linutrition.com

Chapter II.

7. https://www.healthline.com/health/food-nutrition/quinoa-vs-rice#4

8. https://www.mayoclinic.org/diseases-conditions/high-blood-pressure/expert-answers/whole-grain-foods/faq-20058417

9. https://www.healthline.com/health/food-nutrition/quinoa-vs-rice#7

10. https://draxe.com/forbidden-rice/

11. https://www.healthline.com/health/allergies/gluten-food-list#foods-to-avoid

12. https://www.glutenfreeandmore.com/news/Is-Buckwheat-Gluten-Free-4558-1.html?s.

13. www.whfoods.com/genpage.php?tname=foodspice&dbid=52

14. https://www.healthline.com/nutrition/foods/sweet-potatoes

15. https://www.thekitchn.com/the-oat-conundrum-are-oats-glu-137074

Chapter III

16. https://www.mayoclinic.org/healthy-lifestyle/nutrition-and-healthy-eating/in-depth/legumes/art-20044278

17. https://www.healthline.com/nutrition/healthiest-beans-legumes#section1

18. https://www.healthline.com/nutrition/healthiest-beans-legumes#section7

Chapter IV

19. https://www.verywellhealth.com/the-benefits-of-bitter-melon-88317

20. https://www.medicaldaily.com/what-okra-ladys-finger-and-6-benefits-adding-medicinal-.

21. https://articles.mercola.com/sites/articles/archive/2016/08/15/health-benefits-of-okra.aspx

22. https://www.fitday.com/fitness-articles/nutrition/healthy-eating/8-types-of-mushrooms-and-their-health-benefits.html

23. https://www.nutrition-and-you.com/lotus-root.html

24. https://www.organicfacts.net/health-benefits/vegetable/lotus-root.html

25. https://www.livestrong.com/.../510629-the-nutritional-benefits-of-wood-ear-mushrooms/

26. https://www.organicolivia.com/.../why-wood-ear-black-fungus-should-be-a-staple-in-...

27. https://www.baizigui.com.my/en/blog/post/12-top-black-fungus-mushrooms-benefits-for-overall-health

28. https://nutritiondata.self.com/facts/vegetables-and-vegetable-products/3034/2

29. https://www.healwithfood.org/health-benefits/gai-lan-chinese-broccoli.php

30. https://www.healthline.com/.../top-10-evidence-based-health-benefits-of-turmeric

Chapter V.

31. https://thewoksoflife.com/chinese-vegetables-asian-leafy-greens/

32. https://www.google.com/search?q=spaghetti+squash.oven&oq=Spagetti+Squash.&aqs=chrome.3.69i57j0l5.5606j0j8&sourceid=chrome&ie=UTF-8

Yu-Shiaw Chen, Ph.D., CN – Biography

Born in Taiwan, Dr. Yu-Shiaw Chen came to America for advanced study. She earned her Ph.D. in Biochemistry from Mount Sinai School of Medicine in New York City. She has worked as a research scientist for various organizations, including Sloan Kettering Cancer Center and Brookhaven National Laboratories. After realizing the importance of nutrition and its impact on health, she transitioned into a certified nutritionist and nutrition educator.

Dr. Chen designed the 12-week program *Healthy Weight for Life,* to help people lose weight and reduce aches, pains, disorders, and dependency on drugs. She published her first book *Healthy Eating Wholesome Living* in 2011, in both English and Chinese. She has been hosting the Holistic Nutrition Seminar in Stony Brook, New York annually since 2013, which includes her lectures on overcoming health challenges with nutritional therapies, along with her homemade plant-based luncheon. In 2018, she released the video *Optimizing Your Nutrition* online*.*

Currently residing in Northern California with her daughter's family, Dr. Chen enjoys plant-based meal-making. In her spare time, she enjoys writing, counseling, and networking.

www.linutrition.com
facebook.com/linutrition